Boundaries as a Divorce Recovery Tool

Empowerment Strategies for your Relationships, Finances, and Health

Jenny Alexander

Jenny Alexander Publishing

Jenny Alexander

Disclaimer:

This publication is meant as a source of valuable information for the reader, however it is not meant as a substitute for expert assistance. If such level of assistance is required, the services of a competent professional should be sought.

Table of Contents:

Jenny Alexander

Dedication

To the reader healing from divorce, may this guide offer you hope for the days ahead.

Introduction

I wish no one had to go through the pain of divorce. Yet for many of us, it's a reality. While recovery may seem overwhelming, it's possible, even when it feels out of reach.

Since this book focuses on boundaries as a recovery tool, let's lay the foundation regarding their importance.

The DivorceProject shared a lovely quote by a poet named Rainer Maria Rilke who said, *"Boundaries are the lines we draw to protect our heart and soul."* After divorce, that kind of protection is so important. But I'd add that we need to protect the whole person, not just our heart and soul. This book will show you how boundaries do that by guarding specific aspects of your life such as your relationships, finances, and health.

Before we dive into these areas, consider the two quotes below that highlight the necessity for boundaries.

Tracee Ellis Ross says, *"To me, self-care does not mean going to the spa. It's learning to say no."*

This tells us that saying no is an essential part of self-care. It doesn't mean you can't go to the spa while you're recovering – you certainly can. But Ross is stressing that saying no when needed is a commitment to your well-being. And that commitment is all the more needed after a divorce.

Another boundary quote by an unknown author says, *"Boundaries: If someone throws a fit because you set boundaries, it's just more evidence the boundary is needed."*

Boundaries as a Divorce Recovery Tool

Boundary setting isn't about popularity; it's about taking care of yourself. It's okay if others don't like your boundaries. It's also okay to focus on you and your needs at this time. It's not selfish. It's essential.

Now that we've determined the importance of boundaries, let's discuss how healthy boundaries benefit us. Among other things, they bring peace, reduce stress, improve self-esteem, protect good relationships, and guard against harmful ones.

How do boundaries do this? A clue is found in Merriam-Webster Dictionary's definition, which says boundaries are *"something that indicates or fixes a limit or extent."* These limits protect our time, energy, and well-being.

If you're curious how boundaries supported me during my divorce, here are examples of boundaries I set: I ended several long-term friendships that were toxic. That was one of the hardest but most liberating decisions I made during my recovery. Likewise, I decided not to continue a relationship with my in-laws. The alternative was too painful.

I also said yes to things that were good for me like building friendships with like-minded believers and nurturing my sense of self.

Learning to fix and indicate my limits made a difference in the level of peace I experienced on a daily basis during a tumultuous time. My self-esteem began to rise while the level of stress decreased. That's because setting boundaries meant I valued myself and my wishes, not just the wishes of others.

The most important area for me to begin setting boundaries was in my relationships. This makes sense because, as Jim Rohn said, *"You are the average of the five people you spend the most time with."* Similarly, the Bible says, *"Iron sharpeneth iron; so a man sharpeneth the countenance of his friend." (KJV)* We need to spend time with people who influence us for good, who encourage and build us up while we do the same for them. Balance in relationships is key.

I also set boundaries with my finances. For example, I stayed with my parents for several months. This wasn't ideal as a middle-aged woman, but it allowed me to save money for a down payment on a condo.

Additionally, every aspect of my health was impacted by divorce so I needed to set limits there, too. Like when I took a personal day from work to take care of my mental health or switched health care professionals who no longer worked for me. Those decisions weren't easy but helped me in the long run.

In a similar way, these three areas influence your recovery and the limits you set can assist your recovery.

In the remaining chapters, we'll explore how to set boundaries in relationships, manage financial decisions confidently, and prioritize your health. All this with the goal of helping you move forward.

At the end of each chapter, you'll find reflection questions you can use to consider your current relationships with boundaries and identify areas for growth.

Boundaries as a Divorce Recovery Tool

As you continue reading, I encourage you to approach each chapter with an open heart and a willingness to reflect on how boundaries can transform your recovery.

Reflection Questions:

1. Reflect on a recent situation where you struggled to say no. What were the consequences?

2. Recall a moment when you successfully set a boundary. What outcomes resulted from that decision?

3. What areas of your life feel most out of balance, and how might unclear boundaries contribute to that imbalance?

4. What are your biggest fears or hesitations about setting boundaries with others?

5. Can you recall a time when someone else set a boundary with you? How did that make you feel, and how did you respond?

6. What would your ideal life look like if you consistently honoured your boundaries and respected the boundaries of others?

7. What strategies could you use to make setting limits easier in the future? (e.g., rehearsing responses, leaning on a support system).

Preface

I care about those who are hurting from divorce because I've been there. I'm so passionate for helping that this is now my third book in my divorce recovery series.

Know that I know about the tears, confusion, sleepless nights, and pain. I remember wondering if I'd ever sleep through the night without waking, heart pounding, from a disturbing dream of my ex. I questioned whether I could ever do normal things again without feeling weighed down by the pain. But over time, I stopped having those dreams. I started living my life without the weight of emotional baggage. Today, the turmoil of divorce is a distant memory, and my life is so much better.

If you're reading this, I imagine you might be wondering if your pain will ever subside or if life can ever feel normal again. I want to assure you it will and it can.

As you probably already know, healing from divorce happens in stages over time with the help of strategies like counselling, support groups, and journaling. Another powerful tool that isn't talked about enough is boundaries. Boundary setting was certainly a vital aspect of my recovery. They helped me regain control of my life and rebuild my self-esteem.

I wrote this guide to show you that boundaries can help you with your recovery. If you're curious and ready to explore how, I'll meet you on the next page.

Chapter 1: Relationships

We've already touched on the importance of relationships and the critical role boundaries play in divorce recovery. Now, we'll dive deeper into how relationship boundaries can benefit you during this challenging time.

Protecting Your Inner Circle

Boundaries help you keep supportive friends close and remove those who drain you emotionally. You need people who build you up—not complainers, manipulators, or those who thrive on negativity and drama.

Letting Go of Toxic Connections

Sometimes, boundaries require letting go of unhealthy relationships. While this can be painful, it's often necessary. I already mentioned how I ended toxic friendships after divorce. It wasn't easy, but it gave me the space I needed to focus on healing and finding better relationships.

Maintaining Moral Boundaries

Knowing your personal values and standards will protect you from harmful relationships. When you're clear about what you won't tolerate—qualities such as dishonesty, manipulation, or abuse—you can make intentional choices about who to allow into your life. After my divorce, I knew I couldn't be close friends any longer with people who were dishonest and manipulative.

Preserving Your Privacy

After a divorce, nosy people may feel entitled to details about your life. Healthy boundaries allow you to safeguard your privacy. You don't even owe an explanation. If someone presses, you can simply say, "That's personal, and I'd rather not discuss it." If they persist, redirect the conversation or politely end it.

Owning Your Emotions and Responsibilities

Boundaries help you separate your emotions and responsibilities from those of others. For example, during my recovery, I blamed myself for my ex's affairs. Over time, I realized his actions were his choice and not my fault.

Avoiding Manipulation

Manipulative people often take advantage of vulnerable individuals like those recovering from divorce. Limit your interactions with them and focus on what's true rather than their distorted narratives. If you need support to counteract their influence, lean on trusted friends or family or seek professional counselling.

Setting Realistic Expectations

Boundaries help you manage expectations for yourself and others. During emotionally challenging times like divorce recovery, you may react more harshly than usual or set unrealistic standards. Be kind to yourself and recognize it's okay to not be your best during recovery.

Recognizing When to Let People In

Boundaries aren't just about saying no; they also help you say yes to the right people. For example, after my divorce, a neighbour invited me to a barbecue. I initially declined, assuming she didn't actually want me there. But when she encouraged me to join, I went and had a good time.

Nurturing Healthy Relationships

By saying no to toxic relationships, you create space to nurture positive ones. Good relationships are essential during recovery. In my case, I leaned on my family's love and support, which was healing in its own right.

Boundaries with Professionals

During times of heartache, you may also need to set boundaries with professionals like counselors or doctors.

Be clear about the help you're seeking. If a professional relationship isn't working, it's okay to make a change. During my recovery, I switched both a counselor and a dentist because the ones I'd been seeing didn't suit my needs any longer. While these decisions were difficult, they reduced my stress.

Jenny Alexander

Boundaries in Dating

When you're ready to date again, boundaries can protect you and/or you and your children from further pain.

Don't rush into dating out of loneliness or desperation. Instead, focus on healing first. Reflect on what went wrong in your marriage so you don't repeat those patterns in future relationships.

Be cautious about introducing new partners to your children. Ensure you're confident in the relationship before taking that step.

Choose partners wisely to avoid unnecessary heartache. If this is an area you'd like to explore further, my book *Stop Settling When It Comes to Love* and the companion workbook *Your Dating Guide* offer additional guidance.

Moving Forward

These guidelines are a starting point for setting boundaries in various relationships during your recovery. While there may be other specific relationships requiring boundaries, the principles remain the same: prioritize your well-being, nurture supportive connections, and protect your peace.

Reflection Questions

1. Which relationships are draining your energy or causing stress?

2. Identify one supportive relationship you could invest more time in. What steps will you take to nurture it?

3. How do you typically communicate your needs and limits in your relationships, and how effective has this been?

4. What signs do you notice in yourself or others when a boundary is being crossed in a relationship?

5. Are your expectations for yourself and others realistic, or are they contributing to unnecessary pressure?

6. Is there a professional relationship you feel hesitant to address? What boundary could improve this dynamic?

7. What is one healthy way you've been managing loneliness, and how could you foster it?

Chapter 2: Finances

Navigating finances while dealing with the emotional pain of divorce can feel overwhelming. However, setting financial boundaries can save you significant stress during this challenging time. By promoting financial health, you can regain a sense of control and confidence.

In this chapter, we'll explore practical financial boundaries that can help you recover with greater ease.

Creating and Sticking to a Budget

A budget is a powerful tool for financial clarity and discipline.

A budget helps you track spending, prioritize essentials, and identify areas where you can cut back.

Start by listing all your income sources and expenses. Categorize them (e.g., utilities, groceries, entertainment) and identify areas for adjustment.

If you have a friend or family member frequently asking for financial help, a budget provides added justification to say no. Politely but firmly explain, "I'm not able to help you anymore; my situation has changed."

Setting Financial Goals

Financial goals give you a roadmap for stability and growth.

Decide what's most important—whether it's building savings, paying off debt, or reducing unnecessary spending.

Set small, manageable goals like saving a specific amount each month or dining out only twice a month.

Achieving financial goals boosts confidence, which is especially valuable during divorce recovery.

Curb Emotional Spending

Divorce often brings emotional turmoil, which can lead to impulsive spending.

Shopping might provide short-term comfort but can harm your long-term financial health.

One way to combat this tendency is to build occasional, modest indulgences into your budget. That can help satisfy emotional needs without overspending. I wish I had done that.

During my divorce, I indulged in "shopping therapy" and though I kept my purchases within my means, the spending wasn't always necessary so had to be reined in at times.

Tracking Your Progress

Regularly reviewing your financial plan helps you stay on track.

Document your financial goals and review them monthly. This reinforces accountability.

If budgeting feels complicated, ask a trusted friend or family member for help. They can offer guidance or encouragement.

Additional Resources

If you're unsure how to get started, consider using free online tools to help create and manage your budget. Using a resource like

Excelx Budget Templates can simplify the process and help you focus on your financial goals.

Reflection Questions

1. Has it been difficult to establish financial boundaries during your recovery? If so, what specific challenges are you facing?

2. Which financial boundaries would help you feel more secure and in control of your finances during this time?

3. What specific financial goals would you like to set for yourself, and how can they guide your healing process?

4. How can you avoid emotional spending during this recovery period? What strategies can you use to manage impulsive purchases?

5. Do you feel confident about your current financial planning? What steps could you take to improve your financial security as you move forward?

6. Are there any relationships in your life that are impacting your finances? How can you set healthy boundaries in these relationships?

7. Have you created a budget or financial plan? If so, how well is it working for you? If not, what steps can you take to correct that?

Chapter 3. Health

Divorce recovery isn't just about emotional healing—it's about taking care of your whole self: body, mind, and spirit. Setting boundaries in these areas can help you stay balanced and focused on rebuilding your life.

Physical Health

Divorce is emotionally draining, which can make it tempting to turn to unhealthy coping mechanisms like binge eating, drinking, or neglecting your physical well-being. While these might provide temporary comfort, they often lead to guilt or harm in the long run.

Commit ahead of time to caring for your body through healthy eating, regular exercise, and adequate sleep.

Recognize triggers for unhealthy behaviours and set limits to avoid them. For example, if you know certain foods or situations lead to binging, plan alternative activities to redirect your energy.

If sticking to healthy routines feels overwhelming, lean on supportive friends or family for encouragement, or seek help from a nutritionist, personal trainer, or doctor.

Your physical health impacts your emotional resilience and ability to cope with stress. By prioritizing your body's needs, you're better equipped to navigate recovery.

Emotional and Mental Health

Healing after divorce requires acknowledging and processing your emotions. Ignoring the pain only prolongs the recovery process.

Boundaries as a Divorce Recovery Tool

Allow yourself to grieve fully. It's okay to cry, feel angry, or be sad. These feelings are natural and part of the healing process.

Set aside dedicated time to journal, meditate, or simply reflect. If needed, seek therapy or join a support group where you can share and process your experiences.

Cultivating gratitude protects against bitterness. Even on tough days, try to find small things to be thankful for—like your favourite meal or a chat with your friend. This can shift your mindset.

If your job allows it, give yourself permission to take a personal day off from work if your stress feels overwhelming. Recognizing when you need a break is an act of self-respect.

Self-Care Strategies

Engage in activities you enjoy, whether it's reading, gardening, or trying a new hobby. And, by all means, if a visit to the spa is within your means, do that too.

Don't be afraid to ask for help around the house if you're struggling to manage everything on your own. You don't have to do it all.

If you struggle with self-care, habit trackers are an example of a resource that could help. You can find free versions online through sites like Canva.

Heart and Mind/Spiritual Health

Protecting what enters your heart and mind is vital for recovery. Divorce often leaves us vulnerable to negativity, which can deepen emotional wounds.

If scrolling through social media leaves you feeling worse, take a break, customize your feed to include uplifting content, or disconnect altogether for a time. After my divorce, I deleted my Facebook account for a few years. Being on there often caused me to feel discouraged.

Pay attention to how TV shows, movies, or books affect you. Avoid content that triggers sadness, anger, or fear, and focus on what uplifts and inspires you. For me, I couldn't watch or read romantic content for several years and that was okay.

Post-divorce isn't an ideal time for making big life changes. Give yourself time to heal before tackling major decisions like moving, switching jobs, or dating. Even in my case, I didn't end those toxic friendships immediately after divorce. It was a year before I ended the first one and several more years before I ended the others. I needed time to realize they weren't good for me.

If you're a Christian, spend time in prayer, meditation, or quiet reflection. These practices can offer comfort and guidance during hard times.

Stay connected with like-minded individuals, such as a church community who can encourage and support you in your journey.

I write from a Christian perspective but if you have a different faith, taking care of your spiritual life applies no matter your beliefs.

Additional Resources

If you're looking for additional ways to process your emotions and promote healing, journaling can help. Online searches can lead you to free journal prompts, recovery workbooks, or guided journals designed for divorce recovery.

Reflection Questions

1. How are you currently setting boundaries to care for your physical health? Are there any areas where you need to improve?

2. When difficult emotions arise, do you allow yourself to feel and process them fully? Or do you tend to push them aside?

3. How do you take care of your mental and emotional health during times of stress or

heartache? What boundaries could help you protect your peace?

4. What self-care practices do you use to help restore balance to your life? Are you making enough time for them?

5. How do you protect your spiritual health during challenging times? What boundaries can you set to nurture your connection with your faith?

6. Are there any behaviours or habits that are negatively affecting your health such as binge eating, lack of sleep, or overworking? How can you create boundaries to address them?

7. How do you distinguish between your needs and the needs of others when it comes to your health and well-being?

8. Have you been neglecting any aspect of your health? What small step can you take today to prioritize your well-being?

Chapter 4. References & Resources

Christian Singles on the Go PLUS: Loss and Recovery Facebook page: www.facebook.com/christiansinglesonthego

Cloud. (2000). Boundaries in Dating: How Healthy Choices Grow Healthy Relationships

This is my husband, Curtis Alexander's, blog with articles for singles from a Christian perspective:
http://view-finder-blog.blogspot.com/?m=0

Curtis Alexander's YouTube Channel: www.youtube.com/@CurtisAlexanderMusic

DivorceCare: www.divorcecare.org

Boundaries as a Divorce Recovery Tool

The Divorce Project. (2024) <u>Setting Healthy Boundaries After Divorce: A Vital Step for Emotional Wellness</u>

Jeffers. (2007). Feel the Fear and Do It Anyway.

Psychology Today. (2024). <u>The Real Long-Term Physical and Mental Health Effects of Divorce | Psychology Today</u>

Psychology Today. (2025). <u>10 Ways That Better Boundaries Can Improve Your Life | Psychology Today</u>

Vogel. (2008). wHispers. When He is so precious even rocks sing.

Epilogue

It's been a privilege to share what I've learned about boundaries and their role in recovery. Boundaries are more than just limits—they're acts of self-care that affirm your worth and protect your peace. You deserve the freedom and empowerment they provide.

Remember, recovery is a journey and each journey is unique. Some heal sooner. Some take more time.

Also realize that the more you practice setting boundaries, the better you'll be at recognizing when you need them. As you progress, you'll likely discover other areas where you need boundaries, areas we didn't discuss. I suggest that's a sign of growth so be encouraged.

Before I let you go, may I ask a favour? If this book has been helpful to you—or even if you have suggestions for improvement—I'd be grateful if you could leave a short review. Your feedback helps me grow as an author and helps others discover my resources.

If you'd like to stay connected, you're welcome to visit my Facebook author page @hopefortheheartbroken or my blog: https://jennyswordsofworth.blogspot.com/

Thank you for letting me be a part of your journey. I wish you strength, peace, and hope as you move forward. All of these are yours to be had.

Jenny Alexander

Acknowledgments

Thank you to my husband, Curtis, for our brainstorming session about post-divorce boundaries and for your continued support.

Thank you, Pamela Nichols, for reading the draft manuscript and offering suggestions for improvement.

Thank you also to Orla Kenney for reading the draft, offering encouragement, and proofreading.

Thank you Andrew Mikelsons for the light edit. It made a difference.

About the Author

Jenny has a story to tell. Her story is one of recovery and hope. Though her unhealthy first marriage ended in divorce, she healed and now thrives. She writes to help others recover from divorce and make better choices when it comes to relationships.

She is a happy housewife and author who lives in Ontario with her husband, Curtis. She loves pursuing creative interests like sketching, playing the violin, and writing. She holds a Masters in Human Services Counselling from Liberty University.

Jenny Alexander

Books by This Author

Divorce Recovery Handbook: Effective Strategies for Healing

Stop Settling When It Comes to Love: Wise Dating Practices for Women

On the Road to Recovery: Overcoming 10 Common Speed Bumps Post-Divorce

Breaking Free from Toxicity: A Relationship Evaluation Guide

Assurance for Your Soul: A Collection of Original Christian Poetry

Imaginative Bible Meditations: Strengthening Family Devotions with Creativity

Jenny has also written word searches, activity books, journals, children's books, and books about self-publishing. For information about her books and new releases, visit her blog at https://jennyswordsofworth.blogspot.com/